Third Edition

1

WORKBOOK
&
SOLO PRACTICE

GUNTHER BREAUX

With Chris Kobylinski

JAZZ ENGLISH 1 Third Edition
Student Workbook and Solo Practice

Gunther Breaux with Chris Kobylinski

2015 Compass Publishing

All rights reserved. No part of this book may be reproduced, stored in a retrieval system, or transmitted in any form by any means, electronic, mechanical, photocopying, recording, or otherwise without prior permission from the publisher.

Acquisitions Editor: Peggy Anderson
Editor: Daniel Deacon
Design and layout: Gunther Breaux

http://www.compasspub.com
email: info@compasspub.com

ISBN: 978-89-6697-859-5

28 27 26 25 24 23
14 13 12 11 10 9 8 7 6 5

I would like to express my gratitude to Chris Kobylinski for his writing and content contribution. His knowledge of American and Korean culture makes this book more interesting, authentic and relevant.

Daniel Deacon's contribution as editor includes much more than editing. His visual and artistic sense, insight, and teaching experience have enhanced this book.

Website: jazzenglish.com

Printed in Korea

CONTENTS

1	FAMILY	8
2	HOBBIES & INTERESTS	16
3	UNIVERSITY	22
4	SHOPPING	28
5	MOVIES	34
6	FOOD & RESTAURANTS	40
7	SPORTS & EXERCISE	46
8	VACATIONS & TRAVEL	52
	ANSWER KEY	58

All human learning can be summed up in three words:
Watch, try, repeat.

Here is where you repeat.
The more you repeat, the more you improve.

PREVIEW

Why use what's in *JAZZ* only once?

This workbook repeats and recycles what's in the main book. Just as in a workout, you use the same muscles in different exercises. You are going to use certain pages in *Jazz* in several different ways.

Variety. And repetition.

Save a tree. Repeat. Recycle. Improve.

Saying the same thing another way:

How do you get good at something?
You do it more than once.

This workbook uses what's in the book again. And again.

Spend less, improve more.

And save a tree.

Each unit in this workbook has six pages.

The first two pages of each unit are your teacher's LECTURE NOTES.

This is great information, but there is just not enough time to cover it all in class.

Explanations are provided for words that can be used in several ways (e.g., *diet, relax, bargain, hassle*) and words that are often misused (e.g., *fun / funny; variety / various; boring / bored*).

Background and details on cultural differences for some of the Vocabulary Vitamins and Cultural Differences are also provided. For example, I explain one of my favorite idioms: Do you know where *cut to the chase* comes from? Movies.

LECTURE NOTES

3

ARTICLES

Some articles in the Longer & Smoother Speaking paragraph on the sixth page of each *Jazz* unit are blanked out. To check your answers, simply turn to that page of each unit.

PREPOSITIONS

Prepositions and duration words in the Conversation Starters are blanked out. To check your answers, go to the second and third pages of each *Jazz* unit. 3Q is the third question. 3A is the answer to the third question.

In the beginning, you will be guessing. But gradually your brain will recognize a pattern, and soon you will be answering more quickly and correctly.

4

LISTENING & PRONOUNCING

This is a fill-in-the-blank activity. It uses the Model Conversation on the fourth page of each unit. You listen and fill in the blanks, and then listen and repeat several times. You can then check the correct answers in the book.

Many of the answers are Vocabulary Vitamins. Listening to and writing down the new vocabulary helps you master it.

Do you want to check your answers AND improve your listening at the same time?

Don't open the book. Play the audio file to check your answers. Simple.

After you check and correct your answers, play the audio file again. Listen, pause, and pronounce. Then record yourself and save the files. At the end of the semester, you can listen to how you sounded at the beginning of the semester. If you don't like to listen to yourself, how do you think other people feel?

5
VOCABULARY WORKOUT

This is a fill-in-the-blank activity. Many units also have a matching exercise. Then there is a listening quiz based on the Vocabulary Vitamins. Go to the website **jazzenglish.com** and download the audio files. Then listen as many times as needed.

The fill-in-the-blank answers are in the back of the book, and you can check the matching answers in your student book.

6
SPECIFIC EXAMPLES

Here, *academic* means *persuasive*. It means trying to convince people that something is right or wrong, good or bad. To persuade, you give evidence—in other words, specific details.

This activity is great.

1. It will help you clarify your thinking and organize your thoughts.
2. Your speaking will get longer and smoother.
3. It will improve your writing and your speaking at the same time.
4. It's TOEFL essay practice. These answers are actually essay outlines: A, B, C.

Just follow the examples and give your own specific examples. It's your life and your details.

In the back of the book, there's an answer key for the Vocabulary Workout
and for the crossword puzzles in the student book.

This is solo practice.
Do it yourself and check yourself. Improve yourself.

1 FAMILY

COMMON MISTAKES
1. When I middle school student,
2. When I was middle school student,
3. When I middle school,
4. I born in 1978.
5. I born in Masan.
6. I never been to Jejudo.
7. We moved ago two years.
8. I lived Anyang for ten years.
9. I play the piano for six years.

10. Did you ever been gone to . . .
11. Have you ever been gone to . . .

AFTER-SERVICE REPAIRS
When I was a middle school student,
When I was a middle school student,
When I was in middle school,
I was born in 1978.
I was born in Masan.
I have never been to Jejudo.
We moved two years ago.
I lived in Anyang for ten years.
I played the piano for six years. (But I stopped two years ago.)
I have played the piano for six years. (And I still play.)
Did you ever go to Jejudo?
Have you ever been to Jejudo?

Right now and forever,  making those mistakes.

DESCRIBING THE PAST
1. When I was a middle school student, we . . .
2. When I was in the eighth grade, we . . .
3. When I was 10, we . . .
4. I used to live in Mok-dong, but we moved when I was 10.
5. I lived in Mok-dong for ten years, from age 3 to 13.
6. When we lived in Anyang, . . .
7. While we lived in Anyang, . . .
8. During the time we lived in Anyang, . . .
9. My mother used to work at Anyang Hospital.
10. My mother used to work for Anyang Hospital.

FAMILY PARTICIPATION
Everyone / Everybody likes kimchi.
All of us like kimchi.
We all like kimchi.
Most of us like kimchi, but my father doesn't.
Some of us are athletic.
A few of us are talented, but my sister isn't.
Only my mother is religious.
None of us are athletic.
We always celebrate Christmas.
We usually celebrate birthdays.
We sometimes take a vacation together.
We never like the same TV program.

FAMILY FOLLOW-UP QUESTIONS
1. When did your family move to Seoul?
2. How long did you live in Busan?
3. Why did your family move so many times?
4. Which city do you like better?
5. Who are you closest to in your family?
6. Is your family close?
7. Do you like . . . ?
8. Who / What / Which is your favorite?
9. Which do you prefer? / Which do you like better?

Generally, when Americans say "cousin," they mean first cousin. They generally use "relative" for more distant cousins.

LECTURE NOTES

babysit, babysitting, babysat If your partner has a brother or sister, then good follow-up questions could be: *Did you ever babysit for your younger brother? Did your older sister ever babysit for you?* Answers might be: *No, I never babysat. I was never a babysitter.*

maternal grandmother = on your mother's side
  She's my grandmother on my mother's side of the family. He's my uncle on my father's side.

white lie A white lie is a small lie that is polite; it does not hurt someone's feelings.
  "Do I look fat?" "No, you look perfect." "Is Song Hey-kyo prettier than me?" "No way!"

ASKING A PERSONAL QUESTION
Do you mind if I ask . . . ?   *If it's not too personal, . . . ?*

RESPONDING TO A PERSONAL QUESTION
That's OK; I don't mind.	=	No problem.
That's personal.	=	I do not want to answer.
No comment.	=	I really do not want to answer.
That's none of your business.	=	You are rude to ask me, and I am giving you a rude answer.

How, What
How do you do? = *How are you?*
What are you doing? = *What are you doing?* (same meaning)
What are you up to? = *What are you doing? What are you about to do?* (Are you doing something bad?)

WHERE DOES SOME KONGLISH COME FROM?
What do you do? = ***What is your job?***
Americans generally ask: (A) **What does your father do?**
Some Koreans do not understand the question. So Americans then ask: (B) **What is your father's job?**
That is correct grammar, but it is still Konglish.
Therefore, gradually, to save time, Americans stop asking (A) and ask only (B).
As a result, Koreans only hear (B) and they think it is correct English.

THINGS YOU MIGHT NEED TO SAY
1. *My parents got divorced when I was 15.*
2. *My parents are divorced, and I live with my mother.*
3. *My parents do not live together, but they are not divorced.*
4. *My father passed away when I was 12.*
5. *My father died when I was 14.*
6. *I only have one grandparent. The rest have died.*
7. *I have no living grandparents. All of them have died.*
8. *My grandparents passed away when I was young. I don't remember them.*

> Note: *Passed away* is more polite and respectful than *died*. *Passed away* implies that someone died of an illness, usually a long illness. If someone was killed in a car wreck, they *died*; they did not *pass away*.

1 FAMILY

1 ARTICLE PRACTICE

ARTICLES

You can try to learn the rules for using articles, but I do not think that will help much.

However, if you do this exercise for every unit, you will get in the habit of using articles correctly.

Gradually, you will get better. In addition, if you can use articles correctly in the eight *Jazz* units, that will help you use articles correctly when talking about other topics.

> 1. Fill in the blanks with an **ARTICLE** (*a*, *an*, or *the*). Some blanks may need no answer.
> 2. Listen to the audio file and check your answers. Then listen again and repeat.

There are six people in my family: my father, mother, two older sisters, one younger brother, and me. I was born and raised in Gwangju, and we moved to Seoul right before I started college. My father is _____ principal at a private high school, and my mother is a housewife. My parents are _____ outdoor type. Every morning they play _____ badminton, and every weekend they go hiking in the mountains. We are all close, and we always take vacations together. My whole family is musically inclined. We all play at least one musical instrument. In fact, my mother used to be _____ piano teacher until she got married.

My oldest sister is married, and she's _____ pharmacist. She has a son and a daughter. My other sister is _____ university senior majoring in chemistry at Hanyang University. She wants to go to graduate school and be _____ professor. My younger brother is a senior in high school, and he's preparing for his college entrance exams. I'm a sophomore English major at Kyung Hee University. I'm _____ outgoing, outdoor, evening person, and my hobby is playing _____ tennis.

ARTICLE hints:

If the noun is unknown, use *a*. If it is known or specific, use *the*.

 *I went to **a** coffee shop yesterday. I went to **the** coffee shop on campus.*

 *I met **a** boy. **The** boy was cute. **The** boy's hair was **a** strange color. **The** color was kind of green.*

The first time the boy is mentioned, he is unknown (*a*). But the second time the boy is mentioned, the speaker is talking about a specific boy (*the*).

 *I went to **a** temple in Kyongju. **The** temple was on **a** mountain. **The** mountain was quite high.*

For doing certain things, you usually go to the same place, so the noun is specific and **the** is used.

 *I went to **the** bank yesterday. She went to **the** hospital. We went to **the** park. I went to **the** cleaners.*

1 FAMILY

PREPOSITION PRACTICE

PREPOSITIONS

Like the rules for articles, the rules for prepositions are difficult to master.

However, if you do this exercise for every topic, you will get in the habit of using prepositions correctly.

Gradually, you will get better. In addition, if you can use prepositions correctly in the eight *Jazz* units, that will help you use prepositions correctly when talking about other topics.

Below are some questions (Q) and answers (A) from the Conversation Starters (pages 19-20).
Certain prepositions naturally occur in conversations, and these are the ones used.

> 1. Fill in the blanks with the correct prepositions (plus *when* and *while*). Several are used more than once.
>   AT   FOR   DURING   IN   OF   ON   SINCE   TO   WHEN   WHILE   8-9
> 2. Listen to the audio file and check your answers. Then listen and pronounce.

1. 3A   Yes. I have four uncles and four aunts ___on___ both my mother's and father's sides.

2. 4A   My father is a high school math teacher in Mok-dong. He's worked there ___since___ forever.

3. 6A   My older brother works _____ Samsung, and my younger sister goes _____ Yonsei.

4. 9A   Once, they took away my phone _____ a month.

5. 10A   I am close _____ my maternal grandmother. She used to babysit me _____ I was young.

6. 11Q   What does your family do _____ Sundays?

7. 12A   I was born _____ Anyang, and we moved to Seoul _____ I was 10.

8. 13A   Yes, my whole family is pretty good _____ music. We all play an instrument.

WHEN and *WHILE* hints:

WHEN is more commonly used for shorter, more definite periods of time, at a certain point in time.
When you are finished, you can leave. I broke my leg when I was 10.
When you go out, take an umbrella because it might rain.
WHILE is commonly used for longer periods of time, or for indefinite periods of time.
When I broke my leg, I was very scared. While I was in the hospital, a lot of friends came to visit me.
While you are out, could you pick up some milk?
While I was in America, my boyfriend was unfaithful.
While my parents were in China, my sister and I got satellite TV! Daddy was not happy.
You could also say, *When my parents were . . .* Using *While* implies that they were in China, well, for a while.

1 FAMILY

 Listening & Pronouncing

1. Play the Model Conversation several times and fill in the blanks.
2. To check your answers, listen to the audio file again.
3. To improve, listen again, pronounce, and record yourself. Then listen to yourself. If you don't like listening to yourself, how do you think other people feel?

Brad   Hi. My name is Brad.

Britney Hi. My name is Britney. Nice to meet you.

Brad   You too. Is this your _____ today?

Britney No, I have a class first _____. What about you?

Brad   This is my first. I'm not a _____. Say, where are you from, Britney?

Britney Originally from Atlanta. I was _____ there. My family moved to California when I was 17.

Brad   _____? How many people are there in your family?

Britney I'm the middle of three. I have an older brother and a younger sister. _____?

Brad   I'm the youngest of four. I have three _____.

Britney Aha, did your father keep trying for a son?

Brad   Yeah, I think that's what happened. The _____ between each of my sisters is about two years, and then between me and my next sister is six years.

Britney I'll bet your _____ love you!

Brad   Oh, yeah. I'm their only grandson. You should see the photos of my 100-day party.

Britney I can imagine. Are you _____ your sisters?

Brad   _____. They're close to each other, but not so much to me.

Britney Are they _____ all the attention you get?

Brad   Not anymore. I think they gave up. Plus, I'm so _____.

Britney [cough] Oh, yeah. Right. I see it now.

VOCABULARY WORKOUT

1. **Fill in the blanks with a Vocabulary Vitamin from page 18.**

1. My sister and I are _____. We call each other at least three times a day.

2. My _____ came from Ireland. My family name is O'Brien.

3. She received a large _____ when her father passed away. He was very wealthy.

4. He's a(n) _____. I'm not sure how we are related.

5. Do you _____ your father or your mother?

6. My _____ is very large. I still have never met some of them.

7. There was some _____ in my mother's family when she was young. I still don't know the exact details because no one likes to talk about it.

8. My uncle is the _____ of the family. He has been married four times and has been in jail twice.

2. **Go to jazzenglish.com, listen to the short dialogs, and choose the best answer. Sometimes there are two good answers. Choose the best one. Then listen and pronounce.**

You will hear a short dialog and then you will choose the best answer.
Here is an example:

Hey Britney, it's only 9 o'clock. Where are you going?
Home. I have to be home by 10 every night, even on the weekends.

Britney's parents are:
a) lenient   b) strict   c) close-knit   d) spoiled   The answer is: (b) strict.

1 It sounds like Britney:
   a) has a curfew
   b) is close to her parents
   c) gets an allowance
   d) has a supportive family

2 Brad's family is probably:
   a) spoiled
   b) foster parents
   c) spread out
   d) musically inclined

3 Brad's family is:
   a) rich
   b) extended
   c) far-flung
   d) supportive

4 Brad's parents:
   a) have a large age gap
   b) have a family feud
   c) are far-flung
   d) have many descendants

5 Brad and his sister are probably not:
   a) far-flung
   b) musically inclined
   c) close
   d) spoiled

6 Brad's uncle:
   a) has an extended family
   b) is musical
   c) is religious
   d) is the black sheep of the family

jazzenglish.com

1 FAMILY

1 ACADEMIC CONVERSATIONS
Why? Because A, B, C.

ACADEMIC FORMAT FOR CONVERSATIONS
Academic format means *persuasive*. It means not just stating an opinion, but giving reasons for that opinion. It means trying to persuade the listener that something is good or bad, right or wrong, fun or boring.
SPECIFIC EXAMPLES: To be persuasive, offer evidence—SPECIFIC DETAILS. At least two or three specific details. It is hard to argue with specific examples.

CONVERSATION FORMAT	ACADEMIC FORMAT
1. Last weekend was awesome.	Last weekend was awesome because A, B, C.
2. My parents are too strict.	My parents are too strict because A, B, C.
3. Harvard, I am wonderful!	Harvard, you should accept me because A, B, C.
4. My favorite movie is Shrek.	Shrek is my favorite movie because A, B, C.
5. I will tell you about my major.	I chose business as my major because A, B, C.
6. I love TGIFs.	TGIFs is my favorite restaurant because A, B, C.
7. My hobby is aerobics.	I love aerobics because A, B, C.
8. Professor, raise my grade, please!	Professor, you should raise my grade because A, B, C.
9. I broke up with my boyfriend.	I broke up with my boyfriend because A, B, C, D, E, F.
10. Daddy, buy me an iPad!	Daddy, you should buy me an iPad because A, B, C.

Imagine this conversation.

Daughter: *Daddy, you are so handsome, smart, and talented!*
Daddy: *What do you want?*
Daughter: *Wonderful father, please buy me a new iPad.*
Daddy: *No.*
Daughter: *Daddy, you should buy me an iPad because:*
  A: I can save money on books—about $300 every semester.
  B: I can make better grades. I can study anywhere, and I can get a scholarship.
  C: I can use it to make presentations and brochures for your company.
Daddy: *Here's my credit card.*

The daughter used specific examples and made a persuasive argument.

This is a great task:	A: It will clarify your thinking. You will organize your thoughts.
	B: Your speaking will get longer and smoother.
	C: It will improve your writing and your speaking at the same time.

1 FAMILY

SPECIFIC EXAMPLES

1. Read the sample answers and write your own. Try to use new vocabulary.
2. If you do not like the question, make up your own and answer it.
3. Give specific examples: names, dates, time, places, amounts, whatever.
4. Why don't you type the answers on a computer and tape them here? That's what A+ students do.

1. **Are your parents strict or lenient?**
   My parents are definitely strict. First, they're very strict about my curfew. I must be home by 9 during the week and by 11 on the weekends. Second, they are fanatical about my grades. If I get a B in any subject, they punish me. Third, my father is really cheap and my allowance is very small.

   _____
   _____
   _____
   _____

2. **Are you close to your brother or sister?**
   I am pretty close to my sister. First, we are only a year and a half apart, so our age gap is very small. Second, we share a bedroom, so we talk all the time. Third, we are both kind of shy, so we get a lot of companionship from each other. She's my sister and my best friend. We have no secrets.

   _____
   _____
   _____
   _____

3. **Is your family talented in music, art, sports, or anything?**
   My family is pretty talented. First, my mother is talented in music. She can play three musical instruments, and she plays the organ at church on Sundays. Second, my father is into sports—any sport. He's a volunteer soccer coach at our middle school. Third, my sister is very artistic. She paints very well. As for me, I am very good at watching TV!

   _____
   _____
   _____
   _____

1 FAMILY

2 HOBBIES & INTERESTS

(don't) have a hobby

I don't have a hobby. I don't really have a hobby. I sort of have a hobby. I kind of have a hobby. I do volunteer work at my church. I'm too busy these days. My hobby is sleeping.

collect, collection

I collect coins. I have a coin collection. My hobby is collecting coins. I have 200 coins in my collection.

belong to, join

I belong to three clubs. (Do not say *I have three clubs.*) *I joined this club I was a freshman. I wanted to join, but they would not let me.*
Follow-up questions: *How many members are in the club? How often do you meet? Where do you meet? Do you really have a meeting or just goof off?*

catch up on, get caught up on

If you get behind on your homework during the week, you can catch up on your work on the weekend. I caught up on my schoolwork last weekend. I got caught up on my schoolwork last weekend. This weekend I'm going to stay home and catch up on my schoolwork.

good at, skilled, talented

My brother is good at tennis. He is skilled at tennis. He is talented in tennis.
Follow-up questions: *Have you ever won a contest? What was the prize?*

Are you any good?

Not really. I'm OK / so-so / fair / not bad / average / better than average / pretty good.

My mother is a good cook. (Never say *good cooker.*)

addicted, addiction, addict

To be *addicted* means to be unable to stop using or doing something, even when it is harmful (e.g., drugs, alcohol, or gambling). Informally, it also means to like something a lot.
My brother is addicted to the Internet. My sister is addicted to her cell phone.
My father is addicted to soccer. He never misses a game. He's an addict.
My friend is addicted to StarCraft. He plays for hours every day.
He's addicted to computer games. He has a computer game addiction.

Types of books and magazines 👉

| **BOOKS** |
| fiction |
| nonfiction |
| biography |
| comic book |
| history |
| humor |
| mystery |
| romance |
| self-help |
| travel |
| **MAGAZINES** |
| fashion |
| fitness |
| movie |
| sports |
| travel |
| *Time* |
| *Newsweek* |

the last time = most recently

The last time does not mean "the worst time." It means "most recently."
When is the last time you went on vacation?

LECTURE NOTES

HOBBY REWARDS
1. Sewing is relaxing. I find sewing relaxing. Sewing relaxes me.
2. Working with children is rewarding. I find working with orphaned children rewarding.
3. It is rewarding to work with children. Being a social worker doesn't pay much, but it is rewarding.
4. My mother finds it fulfilling to help out at church.
5. I get a sense of fulfillment from sewing. Making clothes gives me a sense of accomplishment.
6. My father gets a sense of fulfillment from coaching soccer.
7. Putting together a big picture puzzle gives me a sense of satisfaction.
8. I get a sense of satisfaction when I see my students succeed in life.
9. Running a marathon gives me a sense of accomplishment.

fun / funny; interesting / interested in
If you look up the translations for *fun* and *interesting* in a Korean dictionary, you will get 재미 for both. But in English, there is a big difference between *fun* and *interesting*. Disneyland is fun. A museum, a zoo, an aquarium, or a TV documentary is interesting.

FUNNY	INTERESTING	FUN
movie	book	vacation
TV program	museum	Caribbean Bay
comedian	documentary	birthday
joke	lecture	weekend
story	person	MT

Funny can also mean "strange; odd."
Let's say someone tells you,
Jack is a funny guy.
You can ask, *Funny ha-ha?*
Or, *Funny ha-ha or funny strange?*
This computer is acting funny.
This program is doing funny things.

1. Jim Carrey is funny. He is a funny guy. He is fun to hang around with.
2. This movie is funny. It is fun to go to the movies. *Shrek* was a funny movie.
3. My weekend was fun. I saw a funny movie on Saturday.
4. Rollerblading is more fun than riding a bike. (Not "funner than"!)
5. Caribbean Bay is fun. The story behind *National Treasure* is interesting.
6. That computer game is fun. That aquarium was interesting. So many strange fish!
7. I'm interested in computer graphics. = I have an interest in computer graphics.
8. Are you interested in photography? = Do you have an interest in photography?

Jack is an interesting person. He has had many different jobs in his life; for example, he was a bartender, dancing instructor, radio DJ, and ship captain. And he is talented in many areas: he can draw and paint very well, he is very good at sports, and he plays several musical instruments.

> **Buff** is slang for a person who is really interested in and knowledgeable about something.
> *I'm a movie buff. I watch a movie every chance I get. I know the actors and directors of just about every major movie. I also know a lot of movie trivia.*
>
> *My father is a history buff. He reads history all the time. He mainly likes historical biographies. His favorite channel is the History Channel.*

2 HOBBIES & INTERESTS

2 ARTICLES & PREPOSITIONS

1. Fill in the blanks with an **ARTICLE** (*a, an,* or *the*). Some blanks may need no answer.
2. Listen to the audio file and check your answers. Then listen and repeat.

16

My hobby is taekwondo, and I belong to _____ club here at school. I started taking _____ taekwondo in _____ first grade, so I have been practicing for twelve years. I'm a fourth-degree black belt. In high school, I was on _____ demonstration team. That was _____ lot of hard work, but we won some contests and I have some trophies. Our university club meets once _____ week, but I wish we met more often. If you meet less than three times _____ week, you don't improve. I like _____ taekwondo because it keeps me physically fit, and I get _____ sense of satisfaction that I am very good at something. Also, it is rewarding to help _____ younger kids learn. Taekwondo is kind of _____ team sport in that you practice with a group, but it is also _____ individual sport in that you compete by yourself.

My parents' hobby is _____ badminton. They belong to _____ league at our local health club. They play about twice a week in _____ mornings before work. They have matching uniforms, and they look like _____ campus couple. They are really into _____ badminton. My mother also teaches _____ bible study to children at our church. That gives her _____ sense of fulfillment. She likes helping people.

3. Fill in the blanks with a **PREPOSITION**. 13-14
ALONG   AROUND   AT   DURING   FOR   IN   ON   SINCE   TO   UNTIL
4. Listen to the Conversation Starters and check your answers. Then listen and pronounce.

1. 3Q   Do you belong _____ a club or organization? Is it a school club? A club _____ your major?

2. 4Q   What do you usually do _____ the weekends?

3. 4A   I just relax _____ the house and play with my kids. Or I catch up _____ my work.

4. 7A   My older brother is good _____ sports, and my younger sister plays the piano.

5. 9A   Oh, I won a science project _____ the sixth grade.

6. 10Q How often do you exercise? How often do you sleep _____ noon?

7. 12A Once, I played _____ ten hours nonstop.

8. 13A On Sunday I watch TV _____ about eight hours.

18   *2 Hobbies & Interests*

LISTENING & PRONOUNCING 2

1. Play the Model Conversation several times and fill in the blanks.
2. To check your answers, listen to the audio file.
3. To improve, listen again, pronounce, and record yourself. Then listen to yourself.
   If you don't like listening to yourself, how do you think other people feel?

15

Brad   Hey, Britney. Long time no see.

Britney Yeah. Did you finish the _____? It was hard.

Brad   Homework?

Britney _____.

Brad   Funny, ha ha. So, Britney, do you have a hobby?

Britney Yes, I like to go _____.

Brad   Where do you go?

Britney My sister and I go rollerblading along the _____ near Hanyang University.

Brad   _____. How often do you go?

Britney We go _____, usually on Saturday afternoon. What about you?

Brad   My hobby is soccer. I'm on my _____ team here at school.

Britney What _____ do you play?

Brad   Well, I used to be the _____, but in the last game we lost 8 to 0, so now I just kind of run around and yell.

Britney _____.

Brad   That's OK; I need the _____. How long have you been rollerblading? Are you any good?

Britney I started in middle school. I'm OK. Now I'm working on going _____.

Brad   Do you wear all those _____ pads and _____ and stuff?

Britney _____. Looking good is half the fun. What's your _____ soccer team?

Brad   Manchester United. _____ I look like a young Cristiano Ronaldo.

Britney [cough] Oh, yeah. I see it now.

2 HOBBIES & INTERESTS

Vocabulary Workout

1. **Fill in the blanks with an expression from page 16.**
2. **Match the opposites. An example is done for you.**

The type of hobby you have is related to the type of personality you have. For example, a loner's hobby might be jogging. Therefore, the answers on this page are from the Personality Test on page 16.

1. You're a(n) _____ person. Your room looks like a typhoon hit it.

2. Stop being so _____. You are the best singer in the group.

3. Aw, don't be a(n) _____. Come to the beer hof with us.

4. You usually go to bed at 5 a.m.? Wow, you are a(n) _____.

5. My father has a(n) _____. Whenever he drives, he honks the horn about once a minute.

6. Your boyfriend didn't forget your birthday. He was just too _____ to buy a present.

7. You have to be home before 10 every night? Your parents are _____.

8. You should share the cookies with your friends. Don't be so _____.

1	always on the go		big spender	1
2	cheap		blabbermouth	2
3	early bird		couch potato	3
4	have patience		generous	4
5	keep a secret		joiner	5
6	loner		late	6
7	modest		lenient	7
8	neat		messy	8
9	organized		modern	9
10	party pooper		night owl	10
11	polite		often lose things	11
12	punctual		outgoing	12
13	shy	12	party animal	13
14	social drinker		rude	14
15	stingy		have a short fuse	15
16	strict		stuck-up	16
17	traditional		weekend warrior	17

3. **Listen to the audio files and choose the best answer. Then listen and pronounce.**

1 Brad's girlfriend sounds like she could be:
 a) a morning person
 b) a loner
 c) a weekend warrior
 d) cheap

2 Brad seems like:
 a) a weekend warrior
 b) an evening person
 c) a morning person
 d) a stingy person

3 It sounds like Brad is:
 a) cheap
 b) a party pooper
 c) a big spender
 d) always on the go

4 Brad's girlfriend might be kind of:
 a) modern
 b) traditional
 c) generous
 d) high-tech

5 Brad appears to be:
 a) an indoor person
 b) an evening person
 c) a stingy person
 d) an outdoor person

6 It looks like Brad's hobby is:
 a) doing volunteer work
 b) playing soccer
 c) cooking
 d) singing

jazzenglish.com

20 *2 Hobbies & Interests*

SPECIFIC EXAMPLES

1. Read the sample answers and write your own. Try to use new vocabulary.
2. If you do not like the question, make up your own and answer it.
3. Give specific examples: names dates, time, places, amounts, whatever.
4. Why don't you type the answers on a computer and tape them here? That's what A+ students do.

1. **Why do you like your hobby?**
   My hobby is rollerblading, and I like it for three main reasons. <u>First</u>, I want my hobby to be an exercise so I can kill two birds with one stone. I can do something that interests me and stay fit at the same time. <u>Second</u>, I think rollerblading is graceful. I feel like I'm flying. <u>Third</u>, I like the outdoors, and with rollerblading I can travel along the Han River and sightsee while I skate.

   _____
   _____
   _____
   _____

2. **Are you an indoor person or an outdoor person?**
   I'm an outdoor person. <u>First</u>, I'm never home on the weekends. On Saturdays I meet my friends in Hongdae, and on Sundays I rollerblade. <u>Second</u>, I really like outdoor activities. I go mountain hiking or camping once a month. <u>Third</u>, I just don't like being indoors. I feel like I'm in jail. I need sunshine to feel alive.

   _____
   _____
   _____
   _____

3. **Why did you join your club?**
   I joined the current events discussion club for three reasons. <u>First</u>, most members of the club are upperclassmen, and they can give me tips on how to make good grades and which teachers are the best. <u>Second</u>, all the members are quite smart, and maybe I can get smarter by hanging around with them. <u>Third</u>, I like to be knowledgeable about current events and hear other people's opinions about them.

   _____
   _____
   _____
   _____

2 HOBBIES & INTERESTS

3 UNIVERSITY

COLLEGE & UNIVERSITY

In America, there are two-year colleges and four-year universities. Many two-year colleges are called community colleges or junior colleges.

College is more commonly used in everyday American English conversation than *university* is. *University* is awkward to use in some sentences, so *college* is used instead. For example:
Where did you go to college? = What university did you go to?

Where did you go to university? Where did you go to a university? Where did you go to the university?
All these sound awkward in American English, so *university* is not used in these questions.

What college did you go to? = What university did you go to?
When did you graduate from college? = When did you graduate?
How did you like college? Was college fun? Did you enjoy college?

My son's in college.   Quit your job and go to college.   College tuition is very high.
Bill Gates is a college dropout.   He dropped out of college.

---

take, have
Last semester I took eighteen hours—six courses.   = Last semester I had eighteen hours.
Next semester I'll take eighteen hours—six classes.   = Next semester I will have eighteen hours.
Last semester I took eighteen hours—six subjects.   = Last semester I had eighteen hours.
I have never taken twenty-one hours.   = I have never had twenty-one hours in one semester.
After this semester, I will have taken ninety-six hours.   = I will have completed ninety-six hours.
I would have taken twenty-one hours, but one class was canceled.

PAYING FOR COLLEGE

In America, college loans are available for everyone. Everybody can borrow money to get a higher education. But getting a college loan can require a lot of complicated paperwork, which discourages some students from applying. (It is easier to ask your parents!) Some students graduate from college with large loans to pay back, some as high as $100,000 (even higher for some medical students and law school students).

COLLEGE AND SPORTS

Personal freedom and individuality are prized in America, so sports (in schools and colleges) are used to teach teamwork and competition. Thus, sports are very big in American schools at all levels. College sports are very big business, and football and basketball games are especially popular on TV. A good high school athlete can go to college free with a sports scholarship.

SCHEDULES

At many big American schools, for big freshman classes, you have two options. You can take a course on Monday, Wednesday, and Friday for one hour, or on Tuesday and Thursday for an hour and a half.

LECTURE NOTES

> **COLLEGE LIFESTYLES**
>
> Some universities are big, with fifteen to twenty thousand students on one campus, while some small private colleges have only one to four thousand students.
>
> Some universities are like small towns. Everybody lives on or near campus, and the neighborhood around campus is the center of their social life. The area is filled with restaurants, coffee shops, bars, and stores.
>
> On the other hand, some universities (especially in big, crowded cities) are called commuter colleges. These are big schools, but most students do not live near the school; they live farther away and commute to school (drive or take public transportation). Thus, during the day, the university is a crowded, busy place. But at night, nothing. No night life. No social activities. All the students have gone home.

heavy load, light load If you are taking twenty-one hours, you have a heavy load. If you are taking only nine hours, you have a light load.
I have a heavy load this semester. I am taking a heavy load this semester.

scholarship usually means free tuition. But there are various types of scholarships. Some scholarships might also pay for books and for room and board (housing and food).
I have a scholarship. I got a scholarship.

goof off means to do nothing, or to do something that is pretty worthless.
Stop goofing off and do your homework. I goofed off all weekend.
I'm tired of studying. I'm going to goof off next weekend.

concentrate, focus, focus on
"I don't understand this math problem." "Concentrate. Focus on the common denominator."
"Hey, look at this new website!" "Focus. Finish your term paper first."
This semester I am going to concentrate on my major courses. I am going to get focused.
No more drinking every weekend. I am going to focus on my grades.

short attention span, long attention span If you can study for three hours without stopping, you have a long attention span. If you can only study for thirty minutes, you have a short attention span. Children usually have a short attention span. On long car trips, they are always asking, "Are we there yet?"

volunteer work, community service
physically challenged, mentally challenged
Many Korean students must perform some community service to graduate.
I did my community service last semester at an old-folk's home. I performed my community service at a center for mentally challenged children. I worked with the physically challenged.
(The old word for the mentally and physically challenged is *retarded*, but that word is not used by polite people, although you may hear it used in movies.)

3 UNIVERSITY

3 ARTICLES & PREPOSITIONS

> 1. Fill in the blanks with an **ARTICLE** (*a, an,* or *the*). Some blanks may need no answer.
> 2. Listen to the audio file and check your answers. Then listen and repeat. 21

(1) College life is rough. In _____ high school, I could goof off and procrastinate all _____ week and just cram _____ night before _____ test, and still make good grades. In those days, I wasn't _____ overachiever, but my grades were above average. These days, I'm studying harder, and I feel like such _____ underachiever. In college, _____ courses are harder, _____ teachers are stricter, and _____ grading is harder. There are _____ bunch of brainiacs in my class, and they all have their own clique.

(2) This semester my most important class is French Culture. My major is _____ French, and it's important to learn French culture because language and culture are closely related. We are learning _____ French history, and after the midterm, we will read some French novels and see some French movies. I like history and movies, so that's great. _____ good news is the professor is French; _____ bad news is she assigns a lot of homework.

(3) This semester I'm taking twenty hours, seven courses total. Three are _____ major courses, two required courses, and two elective courses.

> 3. Fill in the blanks with a **PREPOSITION**. 18-19
> AT   DURING   FOR   FROM   IN   ON   SINCE   TO   WITH   UNTIL
> 4. Listen to the Conversation Starters and check your answers. Then listen and pronounce.

1. 1A   I am a freshman and my major is design. I will specialize _____ fashion design my junior year.
2. 4Q   Do you belong _____ a club or study group? How often does it meet?
3. 5Q   Do you cram for exams? Do you study _____ home or _____ the library?
4. 5A   Yes. I never study _____ the last minute. But this semester I will try harder!
5. 6A   _____ Saturdays I goof off, and _____ Sunday afternoons I start getting ready for the week.
6. 8A   I applied _____ four universities and this was my second choice, but I am really happy here.
7. 9A   I had a part-time job last semester, but I quit to concentrate _____ school.
8. 11Q   Has your cell phone ever rung _____ a class? Have you ever fallen asleep _____ class?

LISTENING & PRONOUNCING 3

 20

1. Play the Model Conversation several times and fill in the blanks.
2. To check your answers, listen again.
3. To improve, listen again, pronounce, and record yourself. And listen to yourself.
   If you don't like listening to yourself, how do you think other people feel?

Brad   Wow, Britney, long time no see.

Britney   Yeah, how are you, Brad?

Brad   Tired. Today is my _____. I have classes from 9:00 to 3:00 _____.

Britney   _____.

Brad   Yeah, I'm _____. What's your schedule like this semester?

Britney   I'm taking twenty hours, but I'm thinking of _____ a course.
I have only one class on Tuesday, and it's an _____, so I might drop it.

Brad   What class?

Britney   It's a _____ course in computer programming, but I just don't get it.
I'm not a _____.

Brad   I know what you mean.

Britney   So, how's the rest of your _____?

Brad   Great. I have late morning and early afternoon classes on Wednesday and Thursday,
and I finish at 6:00 on Friday. Just in time _____.

Britney   Party? How were your _____ last semester?

Brad   No comment. It was a conspiracy. All my teachers were _____.

Britney   _____? Wait, didn't you _____ a class because you were absent too many times?

Brad   _____? This semester I'm going to _____ and make straight A's.

Britney   In your dreams. Did you EVER make an A in college?

Brad   Well, excuse me for not being a _____ like you.

Britney   I'm not a _____. I just keep up with my homework. You
_____ all week, party all weekend, and try to _____ on Sunday night.

Brad   _____. Next topic. Do you still live in the _____?

Britney   Yeah, it's really convenient. I hated the _____ to Incheon. And my roommate
is from France, and she's really good at English.

Brad   Is she cute?

3 UNIVERSITY

25

3 VOCABULARY WORKOUT

> 1. Fill in the blanks with a Vocabulary Vitamin from page 34.
> 2. Match the opposites.

1. How many schools did you _____ to? I sent _____ to four schools.

2. I usually pull _____ before every big test.

3. You haven't picked a topic for your paper yet? Why do you _____ so much?

4. I wish I could take more _____ courses, but I have too many _____ courses left to take.

5. I lost my _____. When is our next exam?

6. See that big guy? He's a(n) _____ on the football team.

7. I got a(n) _____, so my _____ is free.

8. My professor would not change my grade, so I went to see the _____.

1	brainiac		goof off	1
2	easy grader		hard grader	2
3	geek, nerd		jock	3
4	joiner		loner	4
5	lenient; easygoing	10	overachiever	5
6	long attention span		party pooper	6
7	party animal		short attention span	7
8	studious; bookworm		slacker	8
9	study		slow learner	9
10	underachiever		strict	10

> 3. Listen to the audio files and choose the best answer. Then listen and pronounce.

1 Brad will probably not:
  a) get a scholarship
  b) remember his syllabus
  c) flunk out
  d) have an excused absence

2 It sounds like Brad:
  a) commutes
  b) lives within walking distance
  c) is in a sorority
  d) is a bookworm

3 Brad is:
  a) an undergraduate
  b) a graduate student
  c) a nerd
  d) a scholarship student

4 Brad is:
  a) an exchange student
  b) a jock
  c) a bookworm
  d) a transfer student

5 Brad:
  a) pulled an all-nighter
  b) flunked out
  c) has a scholarship
  d) lives in a dormitory

6 Brad:
  a) stayed out of school
  b) posted his homework
  c) played hooky
  d) missed the drop-add period

jazzenglish.com

SPECIFIC EXAMPLES

1. Read the sample answers and write your own. Try to use new vocabulary.
2. If you do not like the question, make up your own and answer it.
3. Give specific examples: names, dates, time, places, amounts, whatever.
4. Why don't you type the answers on a computer and tape them here? That's what A+ students do.

1. **Are you a bookworm or a slacker?**
   Well, half and half. In high school, I was a bookworm. I studied all the time. After school, I went to an academy until 10 and then studied at home until 1 a.m. I had no social life. But now, well, I'm a slacker. My brain is just so tired of studying, I think it's rebelling. Nothing I read stays in. So my brain and I are taking a break. I'll take it easy this year, and whatever grades I make, I make.

   _____
   _____
   _____
   _____

2. **Are you a joiner or a loner?**
   I'm definitely a joiner. First, I belong to three clubs and groups: a photography club, my major club, and my church group. Second, I'm on the student council and a class leader in my major. Third, I hate being alone. When I'm alone, I feel like I'm being punished for something. So I'm always around people.

   _____
   _____
   _____
   _____

3. **Are you an idea person or a detail person?**
   Both, actually. I am into website design, and that takes ideas and creativity. These days, I'm learning how to do animation and movie editing for websites. And as you know, making a website or doing any type of computer programming requires a detail person. Everything has to be perfect or the site won't work. So I'm pretty good at visual ideas for a website, and good at the details to get the site functioning.

   _____
   _____
   _____
   _____

3 UNIVERSITY

4 SHOPPING

bargain

It was a bargain (n). = It was bought at a good price.
My mother usually waits until there are bargains. My mother is a great bargain hunter.
My mother usually bargains (v.) with the seller.
I bargained him down. = I negotiated him down. = I haggled him down. = I haggled the price down.

---

cheap, cheap person, cheap item, cheap price

1. *These shoes look cheap. (bad)*
2. *Wow! These Nike shoes are cheap. (good)*
3. *My boyfriend is cheap. He's a cheap person. (bad)*
4. *Don't be cheap. Get your girlfriend a nice birthday present. (bad)*
5. *My boyfriend got some cheap tickets to the Beyoncé concert. (good)*
6. *Their items are cheap. (They could be good items at a low price, or bad items.)*
7. *That's a cheap price. (good)*
8. *These are the cheapest. Those are the most expensive.*
9. *This is cheaper than that. These are more expensive than those.*
10. *This one is not cheap, but it is the least expensive.*

---

convenience, convenient, comfortable

1. *Internet shopping is convenient.*
2. *I like paying my bills online. Going to the bank is inconvenient.*
3. *For your convenience, you can use these free shopping carts.*
4. *I like the convenience of one-stop shopping.*
5. *My sofa is very comfortable. I usually fall asleep while watching TV.*

---

variety, various, vary

1. *The mall has a variety of stores. Dongdaemun has a wide variety of stores.*
2. *They have various styles to choose from.*
3. *They have a variety of brands and a variety of colors.*
4. *All their merchandise is very similar. They do not have a good variety.*
5. *"Where do you usually go shopping?"*
   "It varies. Usually Shinchon, but sometimes Myeong-dong or Apgujeong-dong."

---

wide selection, good selection

Wide selection and *good selection* can be used similarly, but they have a subtle difference.

They have a wide selection; there are many brands, styles, and colors to choose from (e.g., twenty brands to choose from).

They have a good selection; they have every size and color (e.g., twenty styles or fabrics or colors of one brand to choose from).

LECTURE NOTES

SALES TAX
Why is the sales tax four percent in some cities and five or eight percent in others?
Because a particular city might have a one-percent sales tax, the county might have a three-percent sales tax, and the state might have a three-percent sales tax. Thus, in that city the sales tax would be seven percent (1+3+3).
But in a state such as Alaska (which has a lot of money because of its oil), there is no state sales tax. So a city in Alaska might have a two- to four-percent sales tax.

> **GIFT CERTIFICATES & GIFT CARDS** These can be used in the place of money when you purchase an item. They are prepaid and given as a gift to you from someone else.

haggle, haggling Haggling is in between negotiating and arguing.
> *"Don't haggle, Brad. Just pay the price." "But I like to haggle."*
> *Brad is over there haggling with the merchant. They are haggling over the price.*

impulse buyer, impulse shopper, buy it on impulse, impulsive
> *He's an impulse buyer. He's an impulse shopper. He bought it on impulse.*
> To be impulsive is to act without thinking: *We were young and impulsive. We got married at 20.*

perfume, eau de parfum, eau de toilette Perfume comes in three types: *perfume* is strong, *eau de parfum* is watered down a bit (not as concentrated), and *eau de toilette* is watered down even more. Perfume is for women; cologne is for men.

buy a lot, shopping spree, splurge A shopping spree is when you buy many things. To splurge is to spend a lot, perhaps too much.
> *I went on a shopping spree and bought a whole new wardrobe, a bunch of accessories, and some perfume. I splurged on myself.*
> *For my birthday, I am going to splurge at the beauty shop and get a makeover.*
> *I decided to splurge and get a BMW instead of a Ford.*

> **MODEL CONVERSATION**
>
> **dressed up, dress up, dress down** To dress up is to dress well to try to make a good impression; to dress down is to dress casually. If you are going to meet your boyfriend's parents, you dress up. If you are going to buy a new car, you dress down (so they will not think that you are rich and charge you a lot).
> *"Did you dress up or dress down for your blind date?" "I dressed down. I did not want him falling in love with me."*

4 SHOPPING

4 ARTICLES & PREPOSITIONS

> 1. Fill in the blanks with an **ARTICLE** (*a, an,* or *the*). Some blanks may need no answer.
> 2. Listen to the audio file and check your answers. Then listen and repeat. 26

I'm not into clothes that much. That's why I liked _____ school uniforms in _____ high school. I had no clothing decisions to make every morning. I just put on my uniform. Luckily, right after I got accepted to this university, my dad gave me his credit card and told me to go get _____ college wardrobe. I bought mainly jeans and T-shirts, with _____ few dresses and skirts for special occasions. I also like baggy clothes. Tight-fitting clothes make me feel fat, so I always buy _____ things loose. I bought some Nike sportswear in Dongdaemun, but they fell apart after _____ first washing, so now I think they were knock-offs.

My mother is _____ bargain shopper. She'll shop only when there is _____ sale. She's frugal when it comes to _____ clothes, but she'll buy top-quality food and electronics. And she buys top-end cosmetics. My father is _____ big spender on everything except food. He says it all tastes the same to him. It's _____ good thing Mom buys his clothes for him because he has goofy tastes in clothes. Once, he bought this green checkered suit. My mom screamed, "What were you thinking?" That was _____ impulse buy. Dad lied about where he bought it. He said it was at Lotte, but Mom saw _____ local street vendor with _____ exact same suits. That was _____ quiet night at _____ dinner table.

> 3. Fill in the blanks with a **PREPOSITION** or a **DURATION** word. 23-24
>   AT   DURING   FOR   FROM   IN   ON   SINCE   TO   WITH   WHEN   WHILE
> 4. Listen to the Conversation Starters and check your answers. Then listen and pronounce.

1. 1Q   Do you prefer shopping _____ stores or online?

2. 2Q   How often do you go shopping? Who do you go _____?

3. 3Q   What is the most money you ever spent _____ shopping?

4. 3A   Once, I spent 200,000 won _____ a thick winter jacket _____ the Lotte Department Store.

5. 10Q   How many credit cards do you have? What is the last thing you bought _____ one?

6. 11Q   Where did you get your cell phone? What kind is it? Are you satisfied _____ it?

7. 11A   I bought it _____ Techno Mart last month. It was on sale.

8. 16A   I try to, but sometimes it doesn't all fit _____ my luggage when it's time to go home.

LISTENING & PRONOUNCING 4

1. Play the Model Conversation several times and fill in the blanks.
2. To check your answers, listen again.
3. To improve, listen again, pronounce, and record yourself. Then listen to yourself.
   If you don't like listening to yourself, how do you think other people feel?

 25

Brad   Hey, Britney, where are you going?

Britney Shopping. It's a _____, but somebody's got to do it.

Brad   _____. Is little Miss Cheap actually going to spend some money, or will you just spend the whole afternoon _____ again?

Britney I'm not _____, just frugal. I'm not an _____ like you. Remember that girl's T-shirt you bought? Did you ever wear that?

Brad   Hey! The clerk said it was a unisex shirt. _____. Who's paying for your shopping _____?

Britney My father gave me his _____ and told me to get some new clothes for this semester.

Brad   _____. You hit the _____. Where are you going?

Britney Myeong-dong.

Brad   What will you get?

Britney Clothes, shoes, _____, perfume, purses. Whatever's on sale.

Brad   It's your birthday. _____. Buy something you like, even if it's not on sale. You _____ too much.

Britney _____, that's my hobby.

Brad   Give me a break. You're just cheap. Can I come along and watch you in action?

Britney OK, but help me this time. Last time all you did was _____ with the salesgirls.

Brad   _____? I was turning on the charm so they would give you a better price.

Britney If you say so.

Brad   Are you going to go back to the Lancôme Store? I think that _____ likes me. She kept winking at me.

Britney Brad! _____. She's a salesgirl. It's her job to be nice!

Brad   Aha. That explains why the phone number she gave me was _____.

4 SHOPPING

31

VOCABULARY WORKOUT

> 1. Fill in the blanks with a Vocabulary Vitamin from page 42.
> 2. Match the opposites.

1. Great, I've found a dress for the wedding. Now I need some _____ to go with it.

2. For a major purchase like a computer, you should go with a(n) _____.

3. "Can I help you find anything?" "No thanks, I'm just _____."

4. I got _____ at the mall. I thought I was getting a real Gucci, but it was a(n) _____.

5. Wow. Your camera has all the _____.
   It does everything but brush your teeth.

1	baggy		9	bargain shopper	1
2	bargain			brand name	2
3	brand-new			cheap	3
4	generic			splurge	4
5	luxurious			cologne	5
6	one-stop shopping			mom-and-pop store	6
7	perfume			rip-off	7
8	shopaholic			tight	8
9	be frugal			used	9

6. I wanted to fly first-class on our honeymoon, but my wife was too _____.
   However, we did stay at a very _____ 5-star hotel.

7. Check out my car. It's _____. I got it this morning.

8. My sister went on a(n) _____ and spent way too much money. She bought seven pairs of jeans!

> 3. Listen to the audio files and choose the best answer. Then listen and pronounce.

1 Brad's philosophy in life is:
a) to never get ripped off
b) instant gratification
c) shop till you drop
d) good customer service

2 Brad's hat probably looks:
a) tacky
b) top-end
c) brand name
d) fancy

3 Britney has been:
a) browsing
b) buying designer labels
c) getting refunds
d) on a shopping spree

4 It appears that Britney found a great:
a) souvenir shop
b) novelty shop
c) mom-and-pop store
d) convenience store

5 What did Brad just do with the merchant?
a) Get a refund
b) Buy a knock-off
c) Haggle
d) Buy a top-end item

6 Brad had better hope he has:
a) avoided impulse shopping
b) gotten a refund
c) saved his receipt
d) gotten good service

jazzenglish.com

4 SHOPPING

SPECIFIC EXAMPLES

1. Read the sample answers and write your own. Try to use new vocabulary.
2. If you do not like the question, make up your own and answer it.
3. Give specific examples: names, dates, time, places, amounts, whatever.
4. Why don't you type the answers on a computer and tape them here? That's what A+ students do.

1. **Do you prefer to shop in stores or online?**
   I much prefer to shop online. First, shopping in stores is such a hassle. You have to take the subway, which is crowded, and then you have to fight the crowds in the stores. Second, shopping online gives you a much bigger selection. Third, the prices are cheaper online, especially for books and electronics. I buy clothes in stores, but everything else I buy online.

   _____
   _____
   _____
   _____

2. **Are you a bargain shopper or an impulse buyer?**
   Both. I'm an impulse buyer, but only with cheap things. The things are usually so cheap that I cannot use them or wear them. For example, I bought a knock-off Nike T-shirt and it fell apart in the washing machine. Also, I bought a case for my smart phone, but it did not fit the phone. Third, I bought a really cute belt for my new blue jeans, but it was not long enough. I had to give it to a skinny friend of mine.

   _____
   _____
   _____
   _____

3. **Is your father or mother cheap or a big spender?**
   My father is definitely a big spender. First, he is the first-born son, so he always has to pay for meals whenever we go out with the extended family. Second, he only buys prestige brand items. His golf bag cost something like $1,200. Third, he always buys the newest high-tech gadgets. He makes me wait in line to buy the new iPhones when they come out.

   _____
   _____
   _____
   _____

4 SHOPPING

5 MOVIES

boring, bored
    I am bored. You are boring. = I was bored by you. That was a boring movie. Am I boring you?
    Koreans sometimes ask: *Are you boring?* (Heck no!) They should ask: *Are you bored?*

moving, touching, be moved/touched by   Use these words to describe a movie that really affected you.
    August Rush *moved me.*   *It was a moving experience.*   *I was moved by the final scene.*
    Romeo and Juliet *touched me.*   *It was a touching experience.*   *I was touched by the final scene.*
    I was moved by the sermon at the funeral.   *I was touched by his gesture of kindness.*

recommend
    Koreans often say something like: *I recommend that movie to you. I recommend you see that movie.* That is perfect English, but Americans do not commonly say that. To express the same thought, Americans say things such as: *That was a good movie. I really liked that movie. You should see that movie.*

PARODY, SATIRE, SPOOF

parody: 1) a literary or artistic work that imitates the characteristic style of an author, or a work for comic effect or ridicule
          2) a movie that imitates and makes fun of an earlier movie or movies

For example, *Scary Movie* was a parody of horror movies.
Remember the scene in *Shrek* when Princess Fiona beats up ten bad guys with Chinese-style flying martial arts? That was a parody of Chinese martial arts movies. There was also a wrestling scene that was a parody of American wrestling shows.

satire: 1) irony, sarcasm, or sharp wit used to attack or expose folly, vice, or stupidity
         2) imitation (and perhaps humor) used to criticize and draw attention

For example, *Dr. Strangelove* was a satire of the Cold War and Cold War movies. It aimed to show how unnecessary and stupid the Cold War was.

---

plot, theme
    The plot of *The Shawshank Redemption* is that an innocent banker is sent to prison, he makes some good friends, and after about fifteen years he escapes.
    The theme of *The Shawshank Redemption* is that you should never give up hope. Hope is good.

see, watch
    Generally, you *watch* TV and you *see* a movie at a theater.
    I watched TV last weekend. I saw a great movie last weekend.
    What do you want to watch, CSI *or* Friends?
    What movie do you want to see, Gladiator *or* Troy?
    But if you are at home and will watch it on TV: *What movie do you want to watch,* Gladiator *or* Troy?

LECTURE NOTES

> **cut to the chase** hurry up; fast-forward to the interesting part and skip the boring part
> A: *Wow, the president's speech is really boring. When is he going to make the big announcement?*
> B: *Yeah, I wish he'd just cut to the chase.*
>
> Origins: In the old days, movie executives would watch the preliminary version of a movie. If there was too much talking for too long, they would say, "Cut to the chase." It means, "Fast-forward to the next exciting scene."
>
> Old movies generally were more slowly paced. Today's younger generation has a shorter attention span. If nothing exciting is happening in a TV program for a few minutes, they will switch channels. Similarly, today's movie generation has a short attention span. Thus, most movies, especially action movies, have an exciting scene every twenty minutes or so.

BASIC MOVIE QUESTIONS

Where does your favorite movie take place?
  This is not: Where did you see the movie? This is: Where did the scenes in the movie happen?
  Roman Holiday took place in Rome. *Titanic* took place on a ship in the Atlantic Ocean.

When does it take place?
  This is not: When did you see the movie? This is: When did the scenes in the movie happen?
  Braveheart took place in about 1300. *Roman Holiday* took place in about 1950.
  Schindler's List took place during World War II.
  The Sound of Music took place just before World War II.

What time span does it cover?
  This is not: How long was the movie? This is: How much time, or how many years take place IN the movie? For example, *Titanic* (without the flashbacks) took place in, or covered, about three days.
  Roman Holiday covered two or three days.
  Schindler's List covered about five years (the length of World War II).
  Saving Private Ryan covered about five days.

Have you ever seen a movie or TV star in person?
  In person = face to face, or in the same room, or same stadium or concert hall.
  I saw Britney Spears in person—at a concert, that is, not up close.

He's very versatile. = He does not always play the same type of part in movies.
  For example, Arnold Schwarzenegger and Jackie Chan pretty much always play the same part.
  On the other hand, Nicholas Cage and Leonardo DiCaprio are versatile. They play many different kinds of characters.

talent, celebrity
  Koreans use the word *talent* for a person on TV who is not exactly an actor, singer, or comedian. Americans do not use the word *talent* this way. They use *celebrity*. For example, although Paris Hilton is not exactly talented in any way, she is famous. She is a celebrity.

5 MOVIES

ARTICLES & PREPOSITIONS

> 1. Fill in the blanks with an **ARTICLE** (*a, an,* or *the*). Some blanks do not need answers.
> 2. Listen to the audio file and check your answers. Then listen and repeat. 31

I'm _____ big movie fan. My favorite movies are _____ big-budget superhero movies, like Spider-Man, Batman, Iron Man, *and especially* _____ Avengers *series. In* The Avengers *I like the ensemble cast, and in* Iron Man, *I like* _____ chemistry between Iron Man and his secretary. I must say that all _____ plots are kind of predictable: "All starts out good, _____ world gets into great danger, and _____ heroes save the world." Not much suspense there. Now that I think about it, all _____ movies kind of blend together in my memory, so it's hard right now to tell them part—what exactly happened in which movie. All those movies are made according to _____ same formula, I think, to make them _____ good date movies. They have macho guys, big action scenes, *femme fatales, snappy dialog,* and evil villains.

I love all kinds of movies, except for horror movies and especially slasher movies. I just don't get why they make those movies and why _____ people watch them. I also don't get movies about time travel; I just get confused and fall asleep. And I saw Inception *twice and I still don't get it.* Well, once I dreamed I got it, but then I woke up and lost it.

> 3. Fill in the blanks with a **PREPOSITION** or a **DURATION** word. 28-29
>   AT   DURING   FOR   FROM   IN   OF   ON   WITH   TO   WHEN   WHILE
> 4. Listen to the Conversation Starters and check your answers. Then listen and pronounce.

1. 2A   My favorite is *The Pianist* with Adrien Brody. It takes place _____ World War II.

2. 3A   It covers about five years, from the start to the end _____ the war.

3. 5A   The last movie I went to _____ the theater was the new *Avengers* movie.

4. 7A   Let's see. Probably *Dumb and Dumber*. The worst movie was any drama _____ Jim Carrey.

5. 8A   I love going to the movies _____ Techno Mart.

6. 10A I like Brad Pitt and that guy _____ *Thor*, Chris Hemsworth.

7. 11Q Have you ever fallen asleep _____ a movie theater?

8. 13Q Have you ever seen a movie or TV star _____ person?

36 5 MOVIES

LISTENING & PRONOUNCING 5

1. Play the Model Conversation several times and fill in the blanks.
2. To check your answers, listen again.
3. To improve, listen again, pronounce, and record yourself. Then listen to yourself.

 30

Brad   Hey, Britney, how was _____?

Britney   Great. I went to the movies and *The Avengers 12*.

Brad   _____, right? *The Avengers* already has 11 _____? Amazing. How was it?

Britney   Actually, kind of _____. Blah blah blah, special effects, climactic fight, the _____.

Brad   So, why did you like it?

Britney   Well, the characters are evolving, and there is better _____ between the _____. And there was a great _____.

Brad   Well, what was the _____?

Britney   I don't want to _____ for you. Have you seen any good movies lately?

Brad   I saw *Talk to Me Slowly*. It was a _____ movie, and I fell asleep. I wasted my money.

Britney   _____. Do you remember the plot?

Brad   No, but I remember they talked _____. Live and learn. Oh, a few weeks ago. I saw the new _____ movie by Disney. Now that was an awesome movie.

Britney   _____. Why did you like it so much?

Brad   It was so realistic. The _____ was actually an English professor who did not give any A-pluses. Oh, I could so relate!

Britney   _____? Wait. You're _____?

Brad   Yeah, but I had you going.

Britney   Fine. Just for that, I'll tell you the _____ in *The Avengers*. First, there's a new superhero called Confusion Man. He makes people confused.

Brad   Wait, Confucian Man? He _____ calm?

Britney   Confused. He's Confusion Man, not Confucian Man.

Brad   Oh. Yeah, I see. I think. I'm _____.

5 MOVIES

5 VOCABULARY WORKOUT

1. Fill in the blanks with a Vocabulary Vitamin from page 50.

1. I like science fiction. What is your favorite movie _____?

2. *Titanic* began with a(n) _____ to 1912. I don't like that. It gets confusing.

3. I don't like _____ films because they are too gory.

4. Sylvestor Stallone and Arnold Schwarzenegger usually play _____ guys.

5. Natalie Portman usually plays the _____ type—average, normal, not flashy.

6. The fiancé in *Titanic* was a(n) _____ who bullied poor people.

7. My favorite _____ is Kim Hye-soo.

8. *The Shawshank Redemption* and *Lethal Weapon* are good examples of _____.

9. Tom Hiddleston is good as the hated _____ in the *Thor* series.

10. The first *Transformers* was a good _____. The guys like the action, and the girls like the romance.

11. That movie had too many _____. It was very confusing.

12. Robert Downey, Jr., and Gwyneth Paltrow have great _____ in the *Iron Man* movies.

2. Listen to the audio files and choose the best answer. Then listen and pronounce.

1 What kind of movie did they see?
a) A dialog-driven film
b) A slapstick comedy
c) A musical
d) A black comedy

2 They saw a movie about:
a) two buddies
b) puppy love
c) a love triangle
d) coming of age

3 What kind of cast did the movie have?
a) Ensemble
b) Tough guys
c) *Femme fatales*
d) Villains

4 The movie covered a time span of about:
a) three hours
b) thirty years
c) five years
d) three weeks

5 Where did the movie take place?
a) Techno Mart
b) Kangnam
c) Hollywood
d) Tibet

6 What kind of movie did they see?
a) A sequel
b) A film noir
c) A remake
d) A black comedy

jazzenglish.com

38 5 MOVIES

SPECIFIC EXAMPLES

> 1. Read the sample answers and write your own. Try to use new vocabulary.
> 2. If you do not like the question, make up your own and answer it.
> 3. Give specific examples: names, dates, time, places, amounts, whatever.
> 4. Use: *For example*   *Because*   *Half and half*   *However*   *On the other hand*

1. Why is that your favorite movie?

Mamma Mia! is my favorite movie because <u>first</u>, it is a chick flick. It's about women for women. There's no blood or hours of computer animation. <u>Second</u>, I love the music and dancing. There are a lot of great songs. My favorite is "Dancing Queen." <u>Third</u>, I like the tension between the woman's choices: independence and freedom against less freedom and love, which may not last.

_____

_____

_____

_____

2. Who is your favorite movie star?

My favorite movie star is Hugh Jackman. He's my favorite because <u>first</u>, he's multi-talented. I like that. He's won awards for singing and acting on Broadway, and he sang great in Les Miserables. <u>Second</u>, *he is also a great action star. I like his muscles in the* Wolfman *and* X-Men *movies.* <u>Third</u>, *off-screen he is a nice guy, not a prima donna like some big stars. And he's good-looking. And those muscles!*

_____

_____

_____

_____

3. Do you watch movies to learn something, or to escape reality for a while?

I can escape reality by watching TV. I want to learn something from a movie. <u>First</u>, *whenever I can, I try to read the book and then see the movie. I can compare them.* <u>Second</u>, *I like history, so I like historical movies, such as* Gladiator, The Pianist, Saving Private Ryan, *or* The Hurt Locker. <u>Third</u>, *I'm a business major, so I like to see movies about business, such as* Wall Street *and* The Wolf of Wall Street.

_____

_____

_____

_____

5 MOVIES

6 FOOD & RESTAURANTS

MULTI-PURPOSE WORDS

Barbecue can be a way of cooking or an event.
Let's barbecue some steak tonight. Let's have a barbecue tonight and invite our new neighbors.

Diet can be what you eat or a plan to lose weight.
Does your diet contain enough fruits and vegetables? You have an unhealthy diet. You should eat more seafood and cereals. I'm ten pounds overweight. I'm going to go on a diet (eat less).
I am tired of dieting. I want to get a pizza. I'm dieting now so that I can eat whatever I want on vacation.
A *crash diet* is when you suddenly and immediately eat a lot less. It is not a gradual process. It is a quick, major change in behavior. Crash dieting works in the short term, but it is unhealthy.
I went on a crash diet of only cereal and milk and lost twenty pounds in a month.

Fast food usually means food from McDonald's and similar places.
Junk food is unhealthy food, and fast food is usually unhealthy.

A **chocoholic** loves chocolate. An *alcoholic* loves alcohol. A *workaholic* loves their work, or at least works a lot. Thus, *-aholic* can be added to any word to make it mean that it is loved.
A *chipaholic* loves chips, like potato chips. A *napaholic* loves to take naps. Strangely, you never hear of a *studyholic*.
(The ending *-aholic* can also mean "addict," but its more common meaning is "someone who really likes [something].")

Raw, rare, medium rare, medium, well-done, and **burnt** are terms for how long or how well you would like your steak cooked. *Raw* and *burnt* are exaggerations; nobody really wants to eat raw meat or burned meat.
How do you like your steak? = *How would you like it cooked?* (Rare, medium, well-done?)

WORDS THAT MIGHT BE CONFUSING

spicy and **hot** *Spicy* always means spicy, having a strong (good) taste. *Hot* is sometimes used to mean *spicy: I like hot curry.*
But *hot* can also refer to temperature: *This food is too hot. I like spicy food, but I cannot eat food that is piping hot.*

DISTASTEFUL WORDS

Throw up The scientific term is *vomit*. Slang terms include *barf* (what it sounds like), *upchuck, lose your lunch,* and *toss your cookies.*

Lecture Notes

home cooking, home-cooked meal
After a hard day's work, my father likes a home-cooked meal. My father likes home cooking, but my mother works too, and she would rather eat out.

neighborhood
A neighborhood is similar to a Korean dong, but smaller. Your neighborhood is the area around your house for a few blocks in every direction.
There's a McDonald's and a Popeye's in my neighborhood.
My neighborhood is quiet and safe. It also has a lot of good restaurants.

fancy, ritzy, swanky
Fancy means very nice. Ritzy is nice and expensive. Swanky is nice and very expensive.
I want to go to a fancy restaurant for my birthday. That ritzy restaurant is too expensive for me.
He took me to a swanky restaurant, and then he could not read the menu because it was in French.

pub
Pub is not an American word; it is British English for a small, old-fashioned, neighborhood drinking place. America does not have beer hofs like in Korea. The closest thing might be a sports bar.

skip
I usually skip breakfast. I never have time for it because I always wake up late.
On Wednesdays I have to skip lunch because I have three classes back to back.

foodie, gourmet, connoisseur
A foodie really likes food. A gourmet enjoys and knows a lot about good food and wine. A connoisseur is a higher degree of gourmet. A connoisseur very much likes and knows a lot about fine things: a food connoisseur, a wine connoisseur, an art connoisseur.
He's a food connoisseur. Don't try taking him to eat at a fast-food restaurant.

MORE CULTURAL DIFFERENCES

1. In a Korean restaurant, the waitress or waiter gives you the menu and walks away, and then comes back after you decide what you want. If you order beer or alcohol, they will bring that with the food. In America, they give you the menu and ask if you would like something to drink. You then order your drinks, and they go to get them. By the time they come back with the drinks, you know what you want to eat and you order. This way, you can drink and chat while you are waiting for your food.

2. In a Korean restaurant, the food is usually prepared quickly, within five or ten minutes. In America, the food usually takes longer to prepare, maybe ten to twenty minutes. Thus, the customers will get hungry (and maybe cranky) while waiting so long for their food. Thus, American restaurants usually have some kind of appetizer to snack on while you wait—for example, bread or crackers.

3. In a Korean beer hof, *soju bang*, or restaurant, if you run out of food before you finish drinking, you order some more food. Basically, in Korea, as long as you are drinking, you get food to eat. In America, after the food runs out, people just keep drinking. They do not need food to drink.

6 Food & Restaurants

6 ARTICLES & PREPOSITIONS

> 1. Fill in the blanks with an **ARTICLE** (*a, an,* or *the*). Some blanks may need no answer.
> 2. Listen to the audio file and check your answers. Then listen and repeat. 36

   I am not _____ picky eater. I eat anything. I prefer _____ big portions of anything to small portions of fancy food. My favorite Western food is pizza. The thicker, the better. I like _____ super-supreme, deluxe, combo, the works. _____ only thing I don't like on my pizza is corn. I like _____ rice dishes more than noodle dishes such as jajangmyeon. I also like spicy food such as buldak. I like spicy food, but I cannot eat food or drink coffee if _____ temperature is too hot. To be honest, what I really like is junk food. I love chocolate, donuts, and ice cream. Oh, and I love potato chips and bread.

   My second favorite American food is Popeye's crispy fried chicken. We usually get _____ pizza or fried chicken delivered every other Saturday, so my mom doesn't have to cook. On my birthday we usually go to TGIF's. I like their festive atmosphere, but they're kind of expensive.

   On Fridays after class, I usually meet my friends off _____ campus, and we eat out. We usually have Korean food, either chicken or galbi. I don't like to drink because my face turns red, but I enjoy _____ mood. I used to have _____ curfew, but now I can hang out till whenever. When I get home, I always have _____ midnight munchies, so I hope my mom has some leftovers.

> 3. Fill in the blanks with a **PREPOSITION** or a **DURATION** word. 33-34
>   AT   DURING   FOR   FROM   IN   OF   ON   SINCE   TO   UP   WHILE
> 4. Listen to the Conversation Starters and check your answers. Then listen and pronounce.

1. 2A   I eat out every day _____ my way home _____ school, usually kimbap.
2. 3A   Yes, I love buffets. When I go _____ all-you-can-eat places, I eat till I am stuffed.
3. 7A   Once, _____ vacation, I ate some bad seafood.
4. 8Q   What did you have _____ lunch today? What are you doing _____ lunch today?
5. 12A   Not _____ my neighborhood, but near school there's a coffee shop where I meet my friends.
6. 15Q   Do you usually eat breakfast? Where do you eat _____ school?
7. 15A   Rarely. I generally just pick up a snack on my way _____ school.
8. 16Q   Do you like expensive coffee, like _____ Starbucks?

LISTENING & PRONOUNCING

1. Play the Model Conversation several times and fill in the blanks.
2. To check your answers, listen again.
3. To improve, listen again, pronounce, and record yourself. Then listen to yourself.  35

Brad Hey, Britney, have you had lunch yet?

Britney No. I just got out of class, and I'm _____. I have class from 9:00 to 1:00 straight. What about you? Have you eaten yet?

Brad No. I'm _____ too. Do you want to go _____ that new Chinese pizza place?

Britney _____, right?

Brad No, I hear it's the _____.

Britney Maybe next time. Pizza takes _____. I'm hungry now!

Brad _____. What about Mexican food?

Britney Mexican is OK. What place do you have in mind?

Brad There's a new Mexican place right _____. Second floor.

Britney Naah. I've been there. The _____ are small and the food is too _____. And it's expensive.

Brad Well, _____. Do you have any place in mind?

Britney What about that _____ Mexican restaurant? Big portions, low prices.

Brad No, then I'll _____ and fall asleep in my next class.

Britney Whoa. This is getting _____. I'm hungry! Think of something. Chop-chop.

Brad What about a couple of _____ in the coffee shop?

Britney That'll work. Then I should be perky for my afternoon classes. No nodding off.

Brad Which coffee shop? _____. All coffee tastes the same to me.

Britney _____.

Brad _____? I thought you were a coffee _____.

Britney That's only when _____ is buying.

6 FOOD & RESTAURANTS

43

VOCABULARY WORKOUT

1. Fill in the blanks with a Vocabulary Vitamin from page 58.
2. Match the opposites.

1. Look at your shirt and tie. I'll have to wash them again. You are such a(n) _____.

2. Oh, that beer and chocolate did not mix well. I have a(n) _____.

3. I don't want a whole pizza, just something to _____ on during the game.

4. Your diet has too much _____. You need to eat healthier.

5. He studied cooking in Paris for seven years. Don't call him a(n) _____; he's a(n) _____.

6. My brother is a(n) _____; he likes fancy, expensive food.

7. I don't like to go out to eat with her because it takes her too long to order. She's a very _____.

8. Eat up or you'll be having _____ all week.

1	appetizer		bland	1
2	crispy		dark meat	2
3	eat in		dessert	3
4	ethnic food		famished	4
5	fast food		fast food	5
6	nibble		gourmet	6
7	nutritious		greasy	7
8	spicy		high-calorie	8
9	stuffed		pig out	9
10	white meat	2	take out	10

3. Listen to the audio files and choose the best answer. Then listen and pronounce.

1 It sounds like they are in a:
 a) theme restaurant
 b) sports bar
 c) fast-food joint
 d) vegetarian diner

2 It sounds like the food at that restaurant is:
 a) spicy
 b) mouth-watering
 c) bland
 d) fancy

3 It sounds like Brad's diet is mostly:
 a) low-cholesterol
 b) spicy
 c) low-calorie
 d) fast food

4 It sound like Brad:
 a) is famished
 b) is stuffed
 c) is nauseous
 d) has just finished nibbling

5 It sounds like the family has been eating:
 a) leftovers
 b) fast food
 c) finger food
 d) ethnic food

6 Brad has:
 a) an upset stomach
 b) leftovers
 c) a thick pizza
 d) a sweet tooth

6 Food & Restaurants

SPECIFIC EXAMPLES

1. Read the sample answers and write your own. Try to use new vocabulary.
2. If you do not like the question, make up your own and answer it.
3. Give specific examples: names, dates, time, places, amounts, whatever.
4. Use: *For example   Because   Half and half   However   On the other hand   However*

1. **Are you a gourmet or a junk food junkie?**
   I'm definitely not a gourmet. All food tastes great to me, so why pay more for food that all tastes the same? Actually, I'm a fast-food junkie. <u>First of all</u>, I love Burger King and Popeye's. <u>Second</u>, I love Korean fast food, like kimbap and ddeok-bokki. <u>Third</u>, I love any kind of pizza. All my family is the same. We get fried chicken or pizza delivered about twice a week. My mom is not big on cooking.

   _____
   _____
   _____
   _____

2. **What is your favorite Western restaurant or food?**
   My favorite Western restaurant is Tex-Mex Town, because <u>first</u>, I love Mexican food. My favorite is nachos. I could eat nachos for breakfast, lunch, and dinner. <u>Second</u>, I like their service. They get your food and drinks really fast, and the waitresses are pretty and friendly and very chatty. <u>Third</u>, I like the whole atmosphere. The seats are comfortable and the decorations are authentic.

   _____
   _____
   _____
   _____

3. **Are you a picky eater?**
   Well, I have to admit that I am a bit picky. <u>First of all</u>, I don't like vegetables. Something about their smell just isn't right. I know they are healthy, but yuck. <u>Second</u>, I'm picky about rice. I don't like that rice with black beans. And the rice has to be cooked just right. I don't like soggy rice. <u>Third</u>, I need a dessert. If the restaurant doesn't have dessert, I don't go there.

   _____
   _____
   _____
   _____

6 Food & Restaurants

7 SPORTS & EXERCISE

> **aerobic** = using oxygen
> Exercising continuously for an extended period; for example, swimming, jogging, rowing. Aerobic exercise is good for your heart and lungs (your cardiovascular system).
>
> **anaerobic** = without oxygen
> Exercising for a short period of time; for example, lifting weights. (You could lift a heavy weight over your head while holding your breath.)

black and blue
   My leg is black and blue (bruised). *I am black and blue all over after falling down the stairs.*

build, figure
   He has a nice build. He is well built. She has a nice figure.
   muscular; rippling muscles = *Rambo, Terminator*
   wiry = skinny, but with visible muscles

> **the last one picked** = the worst at sports
> When American kids play a team sport, such as baseball and basketball, they sometimes must choose the teams themselves: Who will be on which team? What is a fair way to decide?
> It often works like this: Two captains are chosen. Then the captains take turns choosing players. Captain A chooses a player (the best), then Captain B chooses (the next best). The captains continue choosing until all the players are picked. The last player picked is the worst player. As you can imagine, it can be pretty embarrassing being the last person picked!

loosen up, warm up   To loosen up is to gradually swing your arms and legs around to get full range of movement.
   To warm up is to get the blood flowing to all of your muscles, to prepare your body for exercising.
   The phrases are similar but not exactly the same, although they are often used interchangeably.

cool down   After intense aerobic exercise, such as aerobics and taekwondo, people cool down. That is, they gradually slow down before quitting, to avoid aches and injury.

MACHINES	treadmill, running machine, stairmaster, rowing machine, elliptical machine
WEIGHTS	free weights, barbells, dumbbells, weight machines
EXERCISES WITH WEIGHTS	bench press, military press, incline press, curls
"UPS"	chin-ups (palms facing your face), pull-ups (palms facing forward), sit-ups

workout, work out
   I had a good workout at the gym. Let's go work out at the gym.
   Brad is not here, he's working out at the gym. He's at the gym working out.

OTHER USES: *We dated for six months, but it didn't work out. We tried to work it out but failed.*

sore, ache   *My legs are sore.*   *I am sore all over after falling down that hill.*
   I ache all over.   *My muscles ache.*   *My muscles are sore.*

LECTURE NOTES

SYNONYMS

abs	killer abs	washboard stomach
awkward	uncoordinated	klutzy
drained	exhausted	pooped
graceful	coordinated	fluid
out of breath	panting	huffing and puffing

> **TRACK AND FIELD** = sports done on a track and in a field
> For example: 100- and 200-meter dashes; 400-, 1000-, and 5000-meter runs; relays, hurdles, long or broad jump, high jump, pole vault, javelin throw, discus throw, decathlon (*deca-* = ten; ten sports)
>
> **SWIMMING STYLES**
> breaststroke / backstroke / sidestroke / butterfly / freestyle / dog paddle
>
> **ROLLERBLADING** = inline skating
> Originally, *Rollerblade* was a brand name (like "Coke") of inline skates. But the word became used for all brands of inline skates.
> Let's go rollerblading. = Let's go inline skating.

fit, in shape, out of shape, in good shape, shapely

You're looking fit. Have you been working out? I feel like an old man. I need to get in shape.
I can't run twenty yards without huffing and puffing. I'm out of shape.
You're still in shape. How do you do it? You're in great shape. You're in awful shape.
Our aerobics instructor has a nice shape. She is shapely. She has a shapely figure.
Note: You can be in good shape (physically fit), but not look like you are in shape (if you are naturally skinny or stocky).

health club, fitness center, health center, club membership

I belong to a health club. I go to a health center twice a week. There's a fitness center in the building where I work. My company pays for my club membership. I have a club membership, but I never go.

taekwondo, kumdo, kendo, hapkido, judo, kick-boxing

These are all martial arts. In Korea, you train in a *dojang*, but among English speakers, the Japanese word *dojo* is more familiar. Your master could be called a taekwondo *instructor*, but instructor is not right, because it does not imply enough skill. Americans do not like calling anyone *master* (it reminds them of slavery), so that is not used. Americans would use *master* if there were only about five masters in the world. So *instructor* is used. In Korea, black belts are common. In America, they are less common and thus more impressive.

REAL-WORLD DIALOG DETAILS

Gotcha! (농담) short for: I got you; I fooled you; I tricked you.
   "Tom Cruise is my cousin." "REALLY?" "Gotcha."
   "He said you were pretty." "REALLY?" "Gotcha."

7 SPORTS & EXERCISE

 ARTICLES & PREPOSITIONS

> 1. Fill in the blanks with an **ARTICLE** (*a, an,* or *the*). Some blanks may need no answer.
> 2. Listen to the audio file and check your answers. Then listen and repeat. 41

When I was young, my favorite sport was baseball. I played on _____ Little League team, and I was pretty good. I was _____ pitcher. I played for two years, but then I had to give it up in _____ middle school. These days my favorite sport is soccer, and I play on my department's team. We practice twice a week and play about once _____ month. I'm pretty good in _____ first half, but in _____ second half I am pooped. I need to pace myself better. I'm _____ pretty good player. I can run faster than most, but my kicking is not so straight. (I think the soccer balls are defective.) Soccer helps me stay in shape. But _____ beers after _____ game make me flabby. My goal this year is to get killer abs. That may take dieting and giving up beer. Ah well, no pain, no gain.

I like to watch all kinds of sports on _____ TV: baseball, basketball, volleyball, soccer, tennis, you name it. My favorite teams are _____ LG Twins and _____ LA Dodgers. Anyway, I enjoy sports and exercise. I think they are good for both my physical and mental health.

> 3. Fill in the blanks with a **PREPOSITION** or a **DURATION** word. 38-39
>   AT   DURING   FOR   FROM   IN   ON   SINCE   WHEN   WHILE
> 4. Listen to the Conversation Starters and check your answers. Then listen and pronounce.

1. 2Q   Have you ever participated _____ a contest?

2. 2A   I took taekwondo _____ I was young, and I won several *pumse* contests.

3. 4A   Oh, yes, I have been swimming _____ I was 10.

4. 8A   I went to a soccer game _____ Jamsil Stadium last month. I went with some friends _____ my department.

5. 12Q Are you taking any sports _____ school now? What sport did you take _____ high school?

6. 14Q Did you ever take taekwondo or kumdo _____ you were young?

7. 15Q Have you ever been injured _____ exercising or playing a sport?

8. 16Q If you could be an Olympic champion, what sport would it be _____?

7 SPORTS & EXERCISE

LISTENING & PRONOUNCING

1. Play the Model Conversation several times and fill in the blanks.
2. To check your answers, listen again.
3. To improve, listen again, pronounce, and record yourself. Then listen to yourself.

Brad   Hey Britney, you're looking great!

Britney   Thanks, Brad. My New Year's resolution was to get _____.

Brad   Well, you did it. How?

Britney   I took up jogging every morning, and I go to _____ every other day.

Brad   How far _____?

Britney   I run around the park five times—that's about two miles.

Brad   _____ does it take?

Britney   About half an hour.

Brad   Did you use any _____?

Britney   No, I hate _____. I decided to eat what I want and exercise.

Brad   Well, it's working.

Britney   Are you still _____ these days?

Brad   Yeah, I do weights twice a week.

Britney   _____?

Brad   Great. You should see my _____. Feel this arm.

Britney   I'll feel your arm, but keep your shirt on. You must really be into _____ these days.

Brad   Yeah, but I don't know how long I can keep it up. To get any _____, I have to work out so hard that I'm _____ all the next day.

Britney   _____. Well, _____.

7 SPORTS & EXERCISE

Vocabulary Workout

1. **Fill in the blanks with a Vocabulary Vitamin from page 66.**
2. **Match the opposites.**

1. I'm _____. I need to start exercising and eating right. I can't go up one flight of stairs without _____.

2. These new jogging shoes gave me a(n) _____. I hate that.

3. Be sure to _____ and _____ before you start playing.

4. You look very _____. Your arms are so big. Have you been working out with weights?

5. My brother is a(n) _____. He exercises every day and goes hiking every weekend.

6. I want some _____. I'm going to start doing five hundred sit-ups every day.

7. After running my first marathon, my legs were _____ for a week.

8. I'm going to go on a(n) _____ and lose ten pounds in two weeks.

1	awkward		skinny	1
2	beer belly		pull a muscle	2
3	couch potato		pig out	3
4	crash diet		pace yourself	4
5	fit		out of shape	5
6	in shape	5	killer abs	6
7	loosen up		graceful	7
8	muscular		flabby	8
9	sprint		fitness freak	9

3. **Listen to the audio files and choose the best answer. Then listen and pronounce.**

1 **Brad has become:**
 a) a fitness freak
 b) a natural athlete
 c) a club member
 d) a yoga instructor

2 **Brad:**
 a) sprained a muscle
 b) is awkward
 c) is a natural athlete
 d) has a blister

3 **Brad is:**
 a) flabby
 b) on a crash diet
 c) out of shape
 d) a couch potato

4 **Brad is probably:**
 a) out of shape
 b) in shape
 c) awkward
 d) fit

5 **Brad probably:**
 a) has an athletic scholarship
 b) has a beer belly
 c) is a fitness freak
 d) is awkward

6 **Brad should:**
 a) hurry up
 b) loosen up
 c) warm up
 d) pace himself

jazzenglish.com

7 Sports & Exercise

SPECIFIC EXAMPLES

1. Read the sample answers and write your own. Try to use new vocabulary.
2. If you do not like the question, make up your own and answer it.
3. Give specific examples: names, dates, time, places, amounts, whatever.
4. Use: *For example   Because   Half and half   However   On the other hand   However*

1. **What is your favorite sport or exercise?**
   My favorite exercise is jogging. I like it because <u>first</u>, it doesn't cost much money. You need good shoes, but that's about it. <u>Second</u>, it is the quickest way to burn a lot of calories. An hour of jogging burns more calories than tennis or soccer. <u>Third</u>, you can do it anywhere. You don't have to join a fancy health club. Also, I find jogging relaxing. Lifting weights takes too much willpower.

   _____
   _____
   _____
   _____

2. **What is your favorite sports team, or who is your favorite sports star?**
   My favorite team is Manchester United. <u>First</u>, I started watching them when Park Ji-sung played for them. Cheering for him made the games more interesting. I was very proud that a Korean was on the best team in the world. <u>Also</u>, I like their uniforms. <u>Lastly</u>, they are a prestige brand, world-famous.

   _____
   _____
   _____
   _____

3. **Do you prefer winter or summer sports? Team or individual sports?**
   Half and half. <u>First</u>, I like winter sports like ice skating because of Kim Yu-na. <u>Second</u>, I like the speed skating events because Koreans are very good at them. Those are individual sports, and I also like summer individual sports such as archery and golf. Koreans are good in those sports. <u>However,</u> I like team sports such as baseball, too. In 2014, the Korean team won the world championship in Little League baseball. Wow!

   _____
   _____
   _____
   _____

7 SPORTS & EXERCISE

8 VACATIONS & TRAVEL

stress, stressful, stressed out
Stress is mental worry and tiredness. When you are very stressed, you are stressed out.
Don't stress; it will be OK. Don't get stressed; it will be OK. Don't get stressed out about it.
You give me stress. You are stressing me out.
I'm stressed out from trying to please my mother-in-law. She stresses me out.
Do you have a stressful job? Air traffic controllers have a stressful job.

> **hassle** To hassle someone is to bother them or to nag them.
> *"Why are your grades so low? Why don't you study?" "Aw, mom, stop hassling me about my grades."*
> *My roommate is always hassling me to help him clean up.*
> *That policeman hassled me because of my long hair.*
> A hassle is a complicated thing.
> *Getting a student loan is a hassle. Too many forms to fill out. I finally decided to just borrow the money from my parents.*
> *Opening up a business is such a hassle. There are so many forms to fill out.*
> *Getting a visa to America is a hassle.*

rip off, rip-off
To be ripped off is to be cheated over price or quality or both. If you pay $400 for a Gucci bag and it turns out to be a fake, you have been ripped off.
They ripped me off (v). This place is a rip-off (n). I was ripped off in the souvenir shop.

rough it
This means to live simply, without a lot of conveniences or luxuries (usually temporarily).
Do you like roughing it? At the Grand Canyon, we decided to rough it and sleep in a tent instead of a hotel.
Grandparents often say: *You kids don't know what "rough" is. When I was your age, I had to walk ten kilometers to school and back every day.*

> **pamper** To pamper someone is to take very good care of them.
> *The resort will pamper you. I was pampered all weekend.*
> *If a child is pampered too much or too long, they will probably become spoiled.*
> *You pamper your child too much.*
> *You are pampering your son too much. No wife will ever pamper him like that, and he will end up divorced.*

sightseeing
Sightseeing has no past tense. You never say, *I sightsaw*. Rather, *I went sightseeing*.
The sightseeing was fun. Let's drive up the coast and go sightseeing.

pension
In America, a pension is your money for retirement.
In Korea, *pension* also means a vacation condo (condominium) or cabin.

LECTURE NOTES

relax, relaxing, relaxation
Relaxing can be mental or physical. Sitting in a hot tub listening to your favorite classical music is relaxing.
Koreans sometimes say, "Take a rest."
Americans do not say that. They say, *Take a break. / Rest. / Relax.*
Sometimes, before a nurse gives you a shot, they say: *Relax, this won't hurt.* (Yeah, right.)
Relax, it will be OK.
I like to relax on the weekend. I like relaxing on the weekend.
Relaxation is very important to both mind and body.

> **travel light**
> *Do you travel light? We traveled light when we went to the Philippines.*
> *I like traveling light. I like to travel light.*

The more the merrier. This means the more people that are involved, the more fun we will have.

theme park = amusement park (because it has a theme, like Caribbean Bay)

get a driver's license In America, each state handles its own driver's licenses. In some states, the minimum driving age is 16, while in other states it is 17 or 18. (When I was young, the driving age in Louisiana was 15, and that's when I got my license.)

semester break, summer vacation, winter vacation
In Korea, the semester break (the time between semesters) is also the summer or winter vacation time. But some American schools have three or four semesters per year, and so the semester break is not always during the summer and winter vacation.

jet lag, jet-lagged *To lag* means to follow behind.
If you leave Seoul at noon and fly for twelve hours, you can land in Los Angeles. When you land, your body will tell you that it is midnight and you should go to sleep. However, it is 9 a.m. in LA, and people are offering you breakfast. In a few days (lag), your body and the local time will be in sync.
My jet lag was really bad on my last trip abroad. I was jet-lagged for a week.

> **rail pass** A rail pass is a train ticket that lets you travel as much as you want, wherever and whenever you want, for a certain amount of time (one or two weeks, or a month).
> Travel by rail is common in Korea and Europe, but it is not as common in America. America is a car culture.
>
> **whiner** To whine is to complain in an annoying way. A person who whines is called a *whiner*.
> *English is too difficult. It's not fair. My head hurts from studying to much. I'm dizzy. My brain is numb.*

8 VACATIONS & TRAVEL

 ARTICLES & PREPOSITIONS

1. Fill in the blanks with an **ARTICLE** (*a, an,* or *the*). Some blanks may need no answer.
2. Listen to the audio file and check your answers. Then listen and repeat.  46

My favorite vacation of all time was _____ last year. My brother and I went to Seattle for _____ month to study English. When that was finished, my parents flew in and rented _____ car, and we drove down _____ Pacific Coast Highway all _____ way to San Diego. We flew home from there. During _____ drive down the coast, my father didn't make any reservations. We would just stop wherever my father chose. _____ scenic route was awesome. Not every motel was deluxe, and we got ripped off _____ couple of times, but it was _____ great adventure. We stayed in _____ bed and breakfast once, run by some old hippies. That was different. We started out traveling light, but we bought so many souvenirs that we had to buy some more luggage to bring everything home. We studied for _____ month, and our road trip lasted ten days. Traffic was great until we got near _____ Los Angeles, and then it was bumper-to-bumper all _____ way to San Diego. Our flight home was great also. My dad arranged it so that we had _____ one-day layover in Hawaii. Aloha!

3. Fill in the blanks with a **PREPOSITION** or a **DURATION** word. 43-44
   AT   DURING   FOR   FROM   IN   ON   SINCE   TO   WHEN   WHILE
4. Listen to the CONVERSATION STARTERS and check your answers. Then listen and pronounce.

1. 2Q   Have you ever traveled _____ abroad?

2. 4A   I visited my grandmother _____ Busan for a month.

3. 6Q   Do you ever get a part-time job _____ the semester breaks?

4. 6A   I usually work _____ a Chinese restaurant _____ my neighborhood.

5. 8A   But I hear it's crowded _____ peak season.

6. 12Q Have you ever gotten lost _____ traveling?

7. 13A I went _____ a school trip _____ Japan when I was _____ middle school.
        We stayed _____ a week.

8. 16A I'll get my driver's license and go _____ a computer academy.

54 **8 VACATIONS & TRAVEL**

LISTENING & PRONOUNCING

1. Play the Model Conversation several times and fill in the blanks.
2. To check your answers, listen again.
3. To improve, listen again, pronounce, and record yourself. Then listen to yourself.

 45

Brad   Hey, Britney, what will you do this winter vacation?

Britney   I have _____ to go visit my aunt in Canada, but it's not certain yet.

Brad   What's your _____?

Britney   I'll stay in Korea and maybe get a _____. What about you?

Brad   I'm going to Europe with a couple of _____.

Britney   _____. How long will you be gone?

Brad   Only for two weeks. It was a real _____ getting the airline tickets. We're traveling during _____.

Britney   I know _____. Where will you go?

Brad   Italy. I like the outdoor scenic views, and my friends like the indoors and _____.

Britney   Are you _____?

Brad   I wish. We have two _____, but those were the only tickets we could afford.

Britney   _____. Be sure to _____.

Brad   We will. We're each taking just one _____. In fact, I'm taking just this _____.

Britney   Good luck with that. Will you get _____ for your phone?

Brad   We all will, in case we get _____.

Britney   I hear that. You _____ a department store.

Brad   Funny. Ha ha. Have you ever been to Italy?

Britney   Yes. It was awesome. Best vacation ever. I only had one bad experience. We were in a hill town _____. I got _____ when I bought an autographed picture of Michelangelo.

Brad   Uh, they didn't _____ in the 1500s.

Britney   Yeah. I know that now!

8 VACATIONS & TRAVEL

Vocabulary Workout

> 1. Fill in the blanks with a Vocabulary Vitamin from page 74.
> 2. Match the opposites.

1. I can't wait until my vacation. After all those problems at work, I really need some _____.

2. Did you bring me back a(n) _____ from Switzerland?

3. That airport gift shop was a(n) _____. This shirt was much cheaper in town.

4. I have _____ to go to Bali, but right now all the flights are booked solid.

5. You should take a long nap. That might help you get over your _____ .

6. My travel agent messed up, and I had a nine-hour _____ in Mexico City.

7. Getting a visa to Nepal was a(n) _____. Next time I'll go to Tibet.

8. Only one small bag? You _____!

1	check in	2	bargain	1
2	convenient		check out	2
3	crystal clear		crowded	3
4	pampered		definite	4
5	peace and quiet		hassle	5
6	privacy		modern	6
7	quaint		noisy	7
8	relaxing		polluted	8
9	rip-off		roughing it	9
10	tentative		stressful	10

> 3. Listen to the audio files and choose the best answer. Then listen and pronounce.

1 It sounds like Brad stayed in a:
 a) bed and breakfast
 b) 5-star hotel
 c) mom-and-pop store
 d) tourist trap

2 It looks like Brad was:
 a) ripped off
 b) hassled
 c) jet-lagged
 d) backpacking

3 Brad took the:
 a) interstate
 b) R&R
 c) scenic route
 d) jet ski

4 Brad likes:
 a) to be pampered
 b) roughing it
 c) bed and breakfasts
 d) waterfalls

5 It sounds like they are:
 a) in a layover
 b) at a waterfall
 c) in a tourist trap
 d) mountain climbing

6 It sounds like Brad is going to:
 a) use roaming service
 b) use his frequent-flyer miles
 c) have a long layover
 d) travel light

jazzenglish.com

8 VACATIONS & TRAVEL

Specific Examples

1. Read the sample answers and write your own. Try to use new vocabulary.
2. If you do not like the question, make up your own and answer it.
3. Give specific examples: names dates, time, places, amounts, whatever.
4. Use: *For example*   *Because*   *Half and half*   *However*   *On the other hand*   *However*

1. **If you could travel anywhere, where would you go?**
   I would go to New York City. First, I want to go to the top of the Empire State Building. I hear the view is fantastic. Second, I want to see Central Park. The park is in many movies and TV shows, and I want to see it in person. Third, I want to visit the Metropolitan Museum. They have some great Van Gogh paintings. Finally, I want to go to a Broadway play.

   _____
   _____
   _____
   _____

2. **What was your best vacation ever?**
   My best vacation ever was last summer when I went to Italy with my family. First, the scenery was beautiful everywhere—in Amalfi in the south, and in the Alps in the north. The Vatican and the Milan Cathedral are awesome. Second, the food was great. I love Italian cooking. Third, the people were very friendly and helpful. They were colorful, authentic people, not like tour guides or greedy merchants.

   _____
   _____
   _____
   _____

3. **Do you like roughing it or do you prefer 5-star hotels?**
   It depends. If I'm in a place like Tibet or Myanmar, I don't want to stay in a fancy hotel. I want to experience the local culture and meet regular people. There is nothing unique or local about 5-star hotels. However, if I am in a big city like London or Paris, I absolutely want to stay in the best hotel possible.

   _____
   _____
   _____
   _____

8 Vacations & Travel

Crossword Puzzle Answers

1 Family
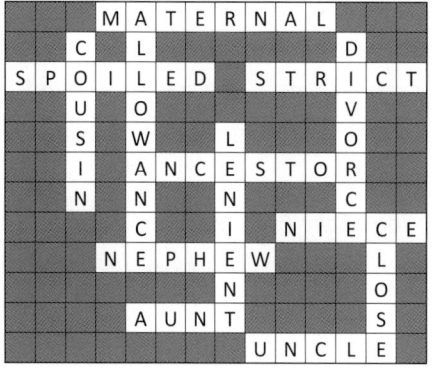

2 Hobbies
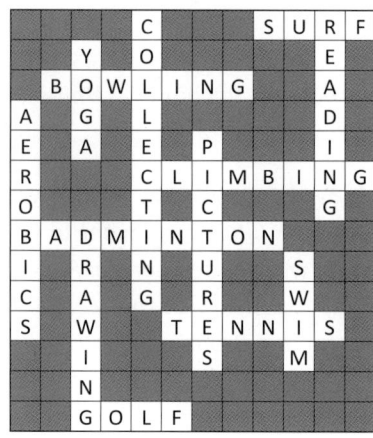

3 University

4 Shopping
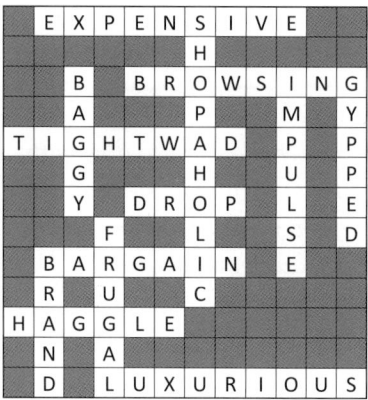

5 Movies
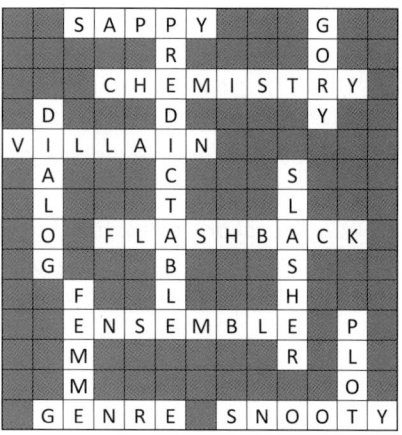

6 Food
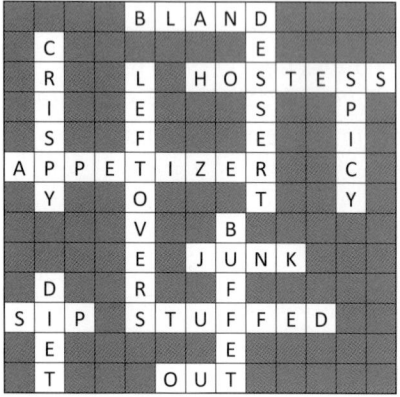

7 Sports

8 Vacations

VOCABULARY WORKOUT
Fill-in-the-Blank Answers

1 FAMILY
1. close
2. ancestors
3. inheritance
4. distant relative
5. take after / favor
6. extended family
7. scandal
8. black sheep

2 HOBBIES & INTERESTS
1. messy
2. modest
3. party pooper
4. night owl
5. short fuse
6. cheap
7. strict
8. stingy

3 UNIVERSITY
1. apply, applications
2. an all-nighter
3. procrastinate
4. elective, required
5. syllabus
6. jock
7. scholarship, tuition
8. dean

4 SHOPPING
1. accessories
2. brand name
3. browsing
4. ripped off, knock-off
5. bells and whistles
6. cheap, luxurious
7. brand-new
8. shopping spree

5 MOVIES
1. genre
2. flashback
3. slasher
4. macho / tough
5. girl-next-door
6. snooty rich type
7. *femme fatale*
8. buddy films
9. villain
10. date flick
11. plot twists
12. chemistry

6 FOOD & RESTAURANTS
1. messy eater
2. upset stomach
3. nibble
4. junk food / fast food
5. cook, chef
6. foodie / gourmet
7. picky eater
8. leftovers

7 SPORTS & EXERCISE
1. out of shape / flabby, panting
2. blister
3. warm up, stretch
4. muscular
5. fitness freak
6. killer abs
7. sore
8. crash diet

8 VACATIONS & TRAVEL
1. R&R
2. souvenir
3. rip-off
4. tentative plans
5. jet lag
6. layover
7. hassle
8. travel light